World-Changing SCIENTISTS

Edwin Hubble

Alix Wood

PowerKiDS press

New York

Published in 2019 by Rosen Publishing
29 East 21st Street, New York, NY 10010

Cataloging-in-Publication Data

Names: Wood, Alix.
Title: Edwin Hubble / Alix Wood.
Description: New York : PowerKids Press, 2019. | Series: World-changing scientists |
Includes glossary and index.
Identifiers: LCCN ISBN 9781538337745 (pbk.) | ISBN 9781538337738 (library bound) |
ISBN 9781538337752 (6 pack)
Subjects: LCSH: Hubble, Edwin, 1889-1953--Juvenile literature. | Astronomers--
United States--Biography--Juvenile literature. | Astronomy--History--
20th century--Juvenile literature.
Classification: LCC QB36.H83 W64 2019 | DDC 520.92 B--dc23

Adaptations to North American edition © 2019
by Rosen Publishing

Produced for Rosen Publishing by Alix Wood Books
Designed by Alix Wood
Editor: Eloise Macgregor

Consultant: Kevin E. Yates, Fellow of the
                Royal Astronomical Society

Photo credits:
Cover, 1 © Johan Hagemeyer/The Huntington Collection, 5 © Andrew Xu; 6 © Webster County
Historical Museum; 7, 9, 10, 14 top, 19 top, 26 top © Adobe Stock Images; 10-11 bottom
© Alfredo Perez; 12 top © Kaofenlio; 13 © ESA/Hubble and NASA; 14 bottom © USDA/USFS; 17, 24,
25 © NASA; 18 © NASA/ESA and the Hubble Heritage Team; 21 © Georg Wiora; 22 © Coneslayer;
23 © Shutterstock; 26 bottom © Dr. Blofeld; 27 top © Alix Wood; 27 bottom © pexels.com; all other
images are in the public domain

Printed in the United States of America

CPSIA compliance information: Batch #CS18PK: For further information contact Rosen Publishing, New York,
New York at 1-800-542-2595.

Contents

World-Changing Scientist
Edwin Hubble

Edwin Powell Hubble (1889 – 1953) was an American **astronomer**, and one of the most important scientists of the twentieth century. His discoveries helped establish the United States as a leading nation in the study of stars, planets, and space. At university, Hubble studied law rather than science, and was a good athlete. His achievements are even more remarkable, as he only concentrated on astronomy later in life.

Science Notes

Edwin Hubble was one of the first scientists to understand that the universe is constantly expanding. Using this knowledge, other scientists have since gone on to discover that the universe must have begun as a result of a large explosion, known as the **"Big Bang."** The force of that explosion is the reason why objects in space are still traveling outward!

In 1924, Edwin Hubble told the world that he had found evidence that our **galaxy**, the Milky Way, was just one of many galaxies. This was a very important discovery at the time, as most scientists believed the Milky Way was the only galaxy. The idea that there might be other galaxies had been suspected by a **philosopher**, Immanuel Kant, as early as 1755. Unlike Hubble, Kant was a philosopher, not a scientist, so he could not prove his theory scientifically.

Despite the opposition, Hubble had his findings published in *The New York Times*, and then presented them to a meeting of the American Astronomical Society. It caused quite a stir!

This photograph is of our galaxy, the Milky Way. A galaxy is a collection of stars, gas, and dust held together by **gravity**. Our galaxy is called the Milky Way because ancient astronomers thought it looked like spilled milk. The whitish glow is actually made by billions of stars!

Edwin's Childhood

Edwin Hubble was born in Marshfield, Missouri, in 1889, the third of eight children. His father, John, was a lawyer. When Hubble's father's eyesight began to fail, he changed jobs to work in insurance. The family moved to the Chicago area. Hubble's father wanted to raise his family away from the city. They lived in Evanston, and later Wheaton, which were quiet suburbs at that time. As John Hubble's health got worse, his company sent him to work in Louisville, Kentucky.

Marshfield, Missouri, in 1895, around when Edwin Hubble would've lived there.

Edwin had a happy childhood. The family were quite well-off and his parents were determined to bring up their children well. Although the Hubble family had servants, they made sure the children did their chores around the house. The children also had to run errands to earn their pocket money.

The family always ate their meals together. The children did their school homework sitting around a large table. On Sundays they would go to church and then Sunday school. The children would spend the rest of the day swimming, riding hay wagons, or sledding, depending on the time of year.

If the weather was bad, the family would play parlor games, or put on concerts for each other. Their father played the violin, and Edwin's sister Lucy played the piano. Edwin and his brother Bill played the mandolin.

a mandolin

A Family Tragedy
Edwin and Bill were close in age and often played together. Their two-year-old younger sister, Virginia, would try to join in, and sometimes break things that the boys were building. One day the boys got quite angry with her. Virginia fell ill some weeks later and sadly died. The boys thought it was their fault and were very upset. Their parents comforted them and helped them get over their guilt.

Edwin Hubble learned to read and write while still very young. He wanted to keep up with his elder brother and sister. His favorite books were adventure stories by Jules Verne and H. Rider Haggard. Young Edwin was also fascinated by astronomy. His grandfather, William Henderson James, was a doctor who loved astronomy, too. He had a **telescope** and Edwin loved to look through it.

Hubble loved looking at the stars. Before Hubble's eighth birthday, he asked if he could not have a party that year, and be allowed to stay up late and look through the telescope instead! His wish was granted. For that birthday, his grandfather bought him a book, *Popular Telescopic Astronomy*, by Alfred Fowler. In the book were instructions on how to build his own telescope!

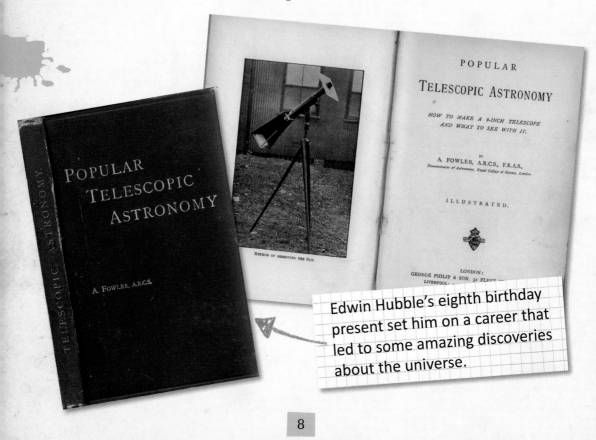

Edwin Hubble's eighth birthday present set him on a career that led to some amazing discoveries about the universe.

Science Notes

Our great space discoveries could not have happened without telescopes. They help us see faraway objects by making them bigger. Telescopes do this by collecting light from distant objects using a lens or mirror. Then, a second lens magnifies and directs the light toward your eye. Try making a simple telescope using two magnifying glasses. Hold one of them over this book. Hold the second one between you and the first magnifying glass. Move the second magnifying glass up and down until the print is in focus. The print will be larger. Do you notice anything unusual about the print?

it's upside down!

Aged 12, Edwin wrote a letter to his grandfather full of questions about Mars. His letter was published in the local newspaper. When Edwin was iil, aged 14, he stayed in bed for as long as possible, so he could read books about the stars. Hubble was good at sports, especially pole-vaulting and basketball, as he was 6 feet 3 inches (1.9 meters) tall by his last year at high school. He was also smart.

At his high school graduation, Hubble's headmaster said: "Edwin Hubble, I have watched you for four years and I have never seen you study for ten minutes." He paused, and then said: "Here is a **scholarship** to the University of Chicago!"

College Life

Following his father's wishes, Hubble studied law at college, although he also took a few science and math classes when he could. He was a strong member of several college sports teams. He played basketball. He once played in a match against his brother, who had gone to the University of Wisconsin.

The university football coach wanted Edwin to join his team, but Hubble's father thought football was too violent. Edwin decided to stress how dangerous his father's favorite game of baseball was, hoping it would help persuade his father to allow him to play football. The idea backfired. His father banned him from playing baseball, too! Edwin took up boxing, and became so good that his coach wanted him to become a professional boxer.

A panorama of the University of Chicago campus as it is today.

Edwin dreamed of winning a Rhodes scholarship and studying in England. Rhodes scholarships were awarded to the best unmarried students aged between 19 and 25 who were healthy, excelled at sports, and had a good character. In 1910, he won a Rhodes scholarship to go to The Queen's College in Oxford.

Just before sailing to England, Hubble went to an astronomy conference at Harvard College. Alfred Fowler spoke at the conference, the man who had inspired him with his book on astronomy. Also speaking at the conference was astronomer Henrietta Leavitt.

Science Notes

Henrietta Leavitt was an American astronomer. She worked at Harvard College Observatory, examining photographic plates to measure and catalog the brightness of the stars. Certain stars pulse in and out, getting dimmer and brighter. Her discovery that there was a relationship between the brightness of such stars and the time it took for them to pulse allowed later astronomers, such as Hubble, to measure the distance between Earth and other galaxies.

Henrietta Leavitt

Edwin spent three years at The Queen's College, Oxford, as one of the university's first Rhodes Scholars. He studied law at first, but after the death of his father in 1913, he added classes in literature and Spanish to his degree.

The quadrangle at The Queen's College, Oxford University.

Needing to support his family after his father's death, Hubble got a job teaching Spanish, physics, and math at New Albany High School, Indiana. He also coached the boy's basketball team. He was a popular teacher.

The Yerkes Observatory's 40-inch (100 cm) refracting telescope, photographed here in 1897, is still in use today!

After a year of teaching, Edwin's brother, Bill, joined the army. Bill's wage meant that Hubble could stop teaching and follow his dream to study astronomy. With the help of his former professor, he got a scholarship to study at the University of Chicago's Yerkes Observatory. Sadly for Hubble, students weren't usually allowed to use the observatory's powerful telescope. Instead, Hubble used a smaller telescope and fitted it with a camera.

Science Notes

Are There Other Galaxies?

While at Yerkes, Hubble went to a talk by astronomer Vesto M. Slipher, who worked at the Lowell Observatory in Flagstaff, Arizona. Slipher was studying **spiral nebulae**. A nebula is a cloud of gas and dust in outer space. Nebulae are visible in the night sky either as a blurry bright patch or as a dark silhouette against the light of other objects. Slipher was beginning to believe that spiral-shaped nebulae were actually other galaxies. Inspired by that talk, Hubble began photographing nebulae. His final essay written while at Yerkes Observatory was called "Photographic Investigations of Faint Nebulae."

Most spiral nebulae are made up of a flat, rotating disk containing stars, gas, and dust.

Going to War

While Hubble was at the Yerkes Observatory, the First World War was raging in Europe. After the United States joined the war in 1917, Hubble rushed to complete his studies and join the Army.

Joining the war meant Hubble had to pass up a great opportunity. An enormous 100-inch (2.5 m) telescope was being installed at Mount Wilson Observatory in Pasadena, California. The director, George Ellery Hale, invited the best American astronomers to work at the observatory. One of those chosen astronomers was Edwin Hubble. Hubble was torn, but eventually sent Hale a telegram saying "Regret cannot accept your invitation. I am off to the war."

Mount Wilson was chosen as the location for the telescope because of the reliable clear weather.

Science Notes

The Hooker Telescope

A new 60-inch (1.5 m) telescope was being installed at the observatory but the director, Hale, decided to go even bigger! He wanted a new 100-inch (2.5 m) telescope that would be able to gather three times as much light as the 60-inch one. The new telescope was named after John Hooker, who donated the money to pay for the construction of its mirror. It took several attempts to make the mirror. The first one, delivered from France, had too many bubbles in it. Two others cracked. A third was too thin. Eventually, Hale went back and decided the first rejected mirror might work. Luckily, it did.

A Sense of Humor

By the time Hubble was sent overseas, the war was practically over. He stayed to do some army office work, and returned home a year later. Hubble enjoyed some of the discipline, but did not completely suit army life. One day, Hubble was riding his bicycle at the drill ground in France when he saw a general. He saluted and said "Good morning, General, nice day, sir." The general was not pleased with this unmilitary greeting. He complained that Hubble should have just given his rank and name and stated what he was doing. Hubble quickly saluted, got back on his bicycle, and rode away, saying, "Sir, Major Hubble, 86th Infantry, getting on his bicycle and riding away."

Discovering Galaxies

As soon as Hubble was back on U.S. soil, he headed to Mount Wilson. Luckily, there was still a job there waiting for him. It was very exciting to use such large telescopes for his research. At the time, most scientists believed that there was just one galaxy in the universe, our galaxy, the Milky Way.

Using the Hooker telescope, Hubble identified a special kind of star in several spiral nebulae that can be used to work out how far away the nebula is. These stars are called **cepheid variables**. Hubble's work proved that these spiral nebulae were too far away to be part of the Milky Way.

Science Notes

How can you tell the distance of a galaxy from its stars ?

Remember Henrietta Leavitt from page 11? The pulsing cepheid variable stars that she studied held the key. Cepheid variables are "standard candles"–that is, stars that have a known brightness. When astronomers compare this known brightness with how bright the stars appear, they can judge how far away they are. Imagine a row of candles lining a path leading away from you. The closer candles will appear brighter, even though all the candles have the same brightness. You can estimate how far away each candle is by how bright it appears.

The Local Group

Edwin Hubble identified our two largest neighboring galaxies, Andromeda and Triangulum. Hubble named these nearby galaxies the "Local Group." At first he believed the group consisted of twelve galaxies. Astronomers have since increased that number to thirty-six, after discovering several galaxies that did not give off much light, and were therefore hard to see.

The Andromeda galaxy, discovered by Edwin Hubble, is larger than the Milky Way.

The Hubble Sequence

Hubble began to study the galaxies. Looking through the powerful Hooker telescope, he began to notice that the galaxies he was studying formed different shapes. Hubble started to classify the galaxies that he saw by their appearance.

Elliptical galaxies are shaped like an ellipse.

Lenticular galaxies are sometimes called armless spiral galaxies. They are disk-shaped, with no spiral arms.

Spiral galaxies have a central bulge with spiral arms coming out from the center.

Barred spiral galaxies are like spiral galaxies, but the arms come out from the ends of a central bar, like ribbons on either end of a baton.

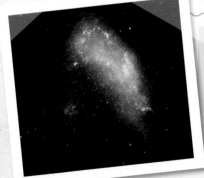

After Hubble's work, scientists have also added another classification, the irregular galaxies. These have no regular shape, and therefore cannot fit into any of the other classes.

Science Notes

Hubble's classification became known as the Hubble sequence. It is also sometimes called the tuning fork diagram, because of the shape of the image used to demonstrate the galaxy types.

a tuning fork

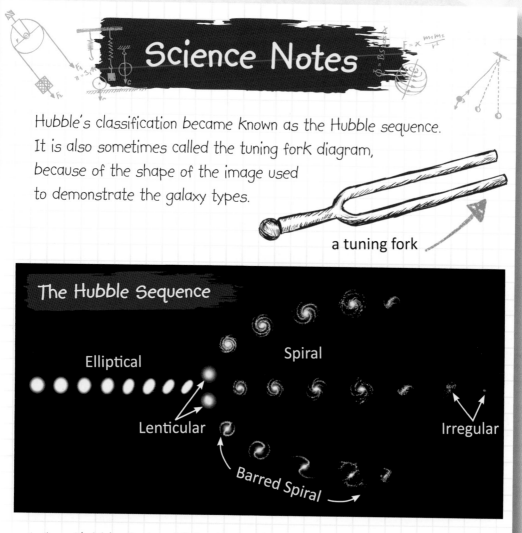

The Hubble Sequence

Elliptical

Spiral

Lenticular

Irregular

Barred Spiral

When Hubble first published his galaxy classification scheme, the existence of lenticular galaxies was just a guess. Hubble believed that there must be a stage between the elliptical galaxies and spiral galaxies. Later, Hubble and other astronomers found some lenticular galaxies, and his belief was proved right. The lenticular class was then added to the Hubble sequence.

The Expanding Universe

Astronomer Vesto Slipher had been studying a phenomenon known as **redshift**. Slipher realized that by monitoring the redshift of objects in space, he could tell the speed that the objects were traveling. Belgian astronomer Georges Lemaître continued this work and realized that as most objects were traveling away from Earth, the universe must be expanding.

Hubble also started to notice that the light coming from the galaxies he studied was shifted a little towards the red end of the **spectrum**. This led him to believe that the galaxies were definitely moving away from Earth. Earlier, Lemaître had worked out a rate at which he thought the universe must be expanding. Edwin Hubble refined the rate a little, and it is now known as Hubble's Law.

Hubble's Law states that the farther away a galaxy is from another point in space, the faster it appears to travel away from that point as the universe expands.

$$v = H_0 D$$

Science Notes

Light acts a little like sound waves. Have you ever noticed that if a police car's siren is moving toward us, the pitch is higher than when it is moving away? This is known as the **Doppler effect**. Light behaves in a similar way, but instead of the sound changing, the color changes depending on if the object is moving closer to us or further away.

What Is Redshift?

Our eyes see the colors of the spectrum. The red end of the spectrum has a lower pitch, or **frequency**, than the blue end of the spectrum. Light from a blue-white star has a high frequency, so the waves of light are closer together. Light from a red star has a low frequency, so its waves are further apart. Just like the siren, as a star moves away, its waves stretch. This makes it appear redder than it really is. If a star is moving closer, the light it gives off gets squeezed together, making it appear bluer than it actually is.

The black lines compare light from the Sun (left) and a distant galaxy (right). The arrows show the galaxy's redshift.

Astronomers know what color light a star should give off. They can work out whether a star is moving toward us or away from us by whether the light is blueshifted or redshifted. Redshifted light means the star is moving away. Blueshifted light means it is moving closer.

The Last Years

In the summer of 1942, Hubble left to serve in World War II. He worked as a civilian for the U.S. Army in Maryland. He was in charge of research in **ballistics**, working on making weapons more effective. He helped develop several pieces of equipment, including a high-speed clock camera, which made it possible to study bombs and missiles in flight. He received the Legion of Merit in 1946 for his work.

When the war was over, Hubble went back to Mount Wilson Observatory. He began work on a new, much larger telescope. The Hale 200-inch (5 m) telescope was to be sited on Palomar Mountain, near San Diego, California. Named in honor of Hubble's old boss, George Ellery Hale, the telescope was four times as powerful as the Hooker. In 1949, Edwin Hubble was given the honor of being the first person to use the telescope.

The dome of the Hale Telescope opening, as night begins to fall.

Hubble had a heart attack in July 1949 while on vacation. He was nursed back to health by his wife, Grace. He died in 1953, from a blood clot in his brain. Oddly, no funeral was held for him, and Grace never told anyone where he was buried.

Science Notes

Hubble and the Sought-After Nobel Prize

Nobel Prizes honor people anywhere in the world who have done outstanding work. The committee at that time did not recognize work done in astronomy. During Hubble's later years, he tried hard to have astronomy considered an area of physics, instead of being its own science. He did this largely so that astronomers might be awarded the Nobel Prize for Physics. Shortly after Hubble's death, the Nobel Prize Committee decided that astronomical work would be eligible for the physics prize. If Edwin Hubble had not died suddenly in 1953, he would have been awarded that year's Nobel Prize for Physics. The prize cannot be awarded to people after their death, so sadly he was never given that honor.

Hubble was honored in 2008 by being featured on a U.S. postal service stamp.

"I knew that even if I were second or third rate, it was astronomy that mattered."

EDWIN HUBBLE

A Great Honor

Edwin Hubble was honored after his death by having a space telescope named after him. In 1990, the Hubble Space Telescope was launched into **orbit** just outside the Earth's **atmosphere**. Our atmosphere is made up of a mixture of gases which distort and block some of the light that comes from space. By positioning the Hubble Space Telescope just outside Earth's atmosphere, it can collect much clearer images of space.

Science Notes

The Hubble Space Telescope completes an orbit around Earth every 95 minutes. It has captured incredible images of faraway galaxies that Edwin Hubble could never have seen using the telescopes that were around during his lifetime. The telescope uses a digital camera to capture its pictures. It then uses radio waves to beam the pictures back to Earth. Scientists then piece the images together so they can study them.

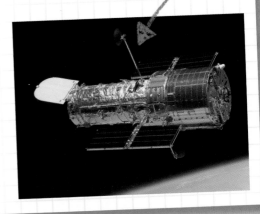

The Hubble Space Telescope

Creating Hubble's Images

The Hubble Space Telescope sends black-and-white images. Color images are created by combining separate black-and-white images taken through different color filters.

One of the Hubble Space Telescope's most famous images, known as *Pillars of Creation*, shows stars forming in the Eagle Nebula.

Science Project

Examining Light Pollution

Why do you think that space observatories are built in remote areas? In a city you may not see as many stars at night as you would in a rural area. Why? Because cities suffer from **light pollution**. Light pollution is the effect of all the light that comes from homes, cars, and streetlights. With so many lights, the city sky never gets completely dark. This can make it difficult to see the stars at night.

Try this project to see what difference light pollution makes in your neighborhood. See if you can find the best place to view the stars.

You Will Need:

- toilet paper tube
- flashlight
- notebook and pen
- a parent or other trusted adult to come with you

1

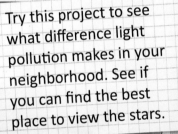

Chose a nice clear night with no full moon. Ask your parents or trusted adult to help you choose four locations. You want some with little light pollution and some with a lot, to compare.

2

Location: Beach Park
Description: Beach by the
 sea with few houses and
 no streetlights

Star Count:

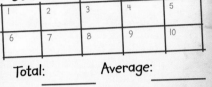

1	2	3	4	5
6	7	8	9	10

Total: _____   Average: _____

Make a table where you can enter your results. You will need space to describe each site, to write ten star counts, and calculate the total and the average star count.

3

Go to the first location with your trusted adult. Use your flashlight to find a safe place to stand. Switch off the light and allow your eyes to adjust to the dark. Look through the tube at an area of sky. Count the stars you can see. Shut your eyes while your adult uses the flashlight to note the number on your table. Look at a new area of sky and repeat until you have 10 results.

4

At each location, repeat step 3. To calculate the average number of stars at each location, add up the total and then divide it by 10. Which location had the biggest tally? Did it match your prediction?

Test Your Knowledge

Test your science knowledge and your memory with this quiz about Edwin Hubble and his work. Can you get them all right? Answers are at the bottom of page 29.

1 What is an astronomer?
a) someone who studies law
b) a scientist who studies the objects in the sky
c) someone who predicts the future

2 Finish this sentence. The universe is ...
a) expanding   b) getting smaller   c) staying completely still

3 What is our galaxy called?
a) Andromeda   b) Triangulum   c) The Milky Way

4 If a star appears redder than it actually is, it is
a) heading away from us
b) heading toward us

5 Did Edwin Hubble win the Nobel Prize?
a) Yes   b) No

6 What do astronomers call a star that has a known brightness?

    a) a shooting star   b) a standard candle   c) a constellation

7 What is the Local Group?

    a) The Milky Way and its nearby galaxies
    b) An astronomy club
    c) Earth's Sun and Moon

8 Finish this sentence. The Hubble sequence classifies ...

    a) telescopes   b) types of galaxy   c) basketballs

9 Why do scientists get such clear pictures from the Hubble Space Telescope?

    a) Because it doesn't wobble
    b) Because it is near a satellite
    c) Because it is outside the Earth's atmosphere

10 What is light pollution?

    a) Pollution that isn't too severe
    b) The effect of artificial light at night
    c) When water is too murky to see through

Answers

1. b – a scientist who studies the objects in the sky; 2. a – expanding; 3. c – the Milky Way; 4. a – heading away from us; 5. b – No; 6. b – a standard candle; 7. a – The Milky Way and its nearby galaxies; 8. b – types of galaxy; 9. c – Because it is outside the Earth's atmosphere; 10. b – The effect of artificial light at night

Glossary

astronomer A scientific observer of the celestial bodies.

atmosphere The whole mass of air surrounding the Earth.

ballistics The science that deals with the motion of objects that are thrown or driven forward.

Big Bang The explosion believed to have caused the beginning of the universe.

cepheid variables Variable stars having a regular cycle of brightness, allowing estimation of their distance from Earth.

Doppler effect An increase or decrease in the frequency of sound, light, or other waves as the source and observer move towards or away from each other.

frequency The number of waves that pass a fixed point each second.

galaxy One of the very large groups of stars and other matter that are found throughout the universe.

gravity The gravitational attraction of the mass of a heavenly body for bodies at or near its surface.

light pollution Brightening of the night sky caused by streetlights and other human-made sources.

orbit To circle around.

philosopher Someone who studies the basic ideas about knowledge, truth, right and wrong, religion, and the nature and meaning of life.

redshift Displacement of a spectrum especially of a heavenly body toward longer wavelengths.

scholarship Money given to a student to help pay for further education.

spectrum The colors red, orange, yellow, green, blue, indigo, and violet in the order of their wavelengths, which may be seen when white light passes through a prism and falls on a surface.

spiral nebulae Galaxies consisting of a flat, rotating disk containing stars, gas, and dust, with a central concentration of stars.

telescope A tubular instrument for viewing distant objects by focusing light rays with mirrors or lenses.

For More Information

Datnow, Claire L. *Edwin Hubble: Genius Discoverer of Galaxies* (Genius Scientists and Their Genius Ideas). New York, NY: Enslow Publishers, 2015.

Goldsmith, Mike. *The Kingfisher Space Encyclopedia* (Kingfisher Encyclopedias). London, UK : Kingfisher, 2017.

Jankowski, Connie. *From Hubble to Hubble* (Science Readers). Huntington Beach, CA: Teacher Created Materials, 2007.

Scott, Elaine. *Space, Stars, and the Beginning of Time: What the Hubble Telescope Saw.* New York, NY: Clarion Books, 2011.

Websites

Due to the changing nature of Internet links, PowerKids Press has developed an online list of websites related to the subject of this book. This site is updated regularly. Please use this link to access the list:

www.powerkidslinks.com/wcs/hubble

Index